CHRISTMAS!

the
whole story
of the
God
who
loves

Published by Olive Press
Messianic and Christian Publisher

Christmas! The Whole Story of the God Who Loves
Copyright © 2015 by Natasha Metzler
Illustrations Copyright © 2015 by Brianna Siegrist

ISBN: 978-1-941173-14-5

www.olivepresspublisher.com

Cover design: Brianna Siegrist, Natasha Metzler

Ordering Information:

Quantity sales. Special discounts are available on quantity purchases by corporations,
associations, and others. For details, contact the publisher at the address above.

CHRISTMAS!

the
whole story
of the
God
who
loves

WRITTEN BY
NATASHA METZLER

ILLUSTRATED BY
BRIANNA SIEGRIST

OlivePress
צהר זית
Messianic & Christian Publisher

for Dominic & Aiden James

MAY YOU ALWAYS FOLLOW
THE GOD WHO LOVES

Dear Parents,

I wrote this book while wandering through the trial of infertility. After fighting with God over my childless state, I finally surrendered and made the choice to trust Him, even though my life was turning out vastly different than what I expected and desired. In the midst of that decision, I started babysitting two little boys and when the holidays arrived, I wanted to do something special for them. I set up an Advent calendar of Christmas activities, and started looking for an Advent book to share with them the greatest love story of all eternity.

Except, I couldn't find just the right one. There were a lot of beautiful and interesting books and would have been amazing… but they were all missing some element I desperately desired.

I wanted a book that started at the beginning and told the story from the moment when only God existed and nothing else. I needed a book that was short and to-the-point, because these rambunctious boys were not going to stay focused for more than a few minutes. And I wanted a book that told the whole story—how Jesus was promised from the garden and everything we learn after that just points us to Him.

When I was unable to find just what I wanted, I decided to write my own. What you are reading now is the outcome of that project. From creation to redemption, *Christmas!* will walk your children through some of the best-loved stories from Scripture and show them how it was all about Jesus and the Father's love from the very beginning.

For the smaller children there are friendly little bugs hidden somewhere in each day's spread—and for older children, there is a "Learn More" section at the end, which encourages them to go back to the Bible for the original stories.

I pray this book will become a family tradition in your home for years to come, and that your children will never forget the most incredible love story in all eternity.

Natasha Metzler

[created]

In the beginning, (I mean, the very, very beginning) there was only one thing.
It wasn't the sun, or the moon, or the stars.
It wasn't animals, or plants, or people.
It was God.
He was before the beginning, during the beginning, and He will be after the end.

That's just the way God is.

And in the beginning, God created the heavens and the earth. Everything was dark. Just dark. But God spoke!

Really great things happen when God speaks.

He said, "Let there be light!" and there was.
He said the light would be called "day" and the dark "night". And He said it was good.

Day after day passed and He made a lot of good things. He made the sky and the seas and all kinds of plants. He made the sun and moon and stars. He made all the fish and birds and animals.

And God said it was all good. The whole world was there and God was pleased with it.

Then God did something very, very special. He said to Himself, "Let us make mankind…" He took the dust of the ground and formed a man and He breathed into the man *the breath of life.*

The man God created, Adam, named all the animals and birds and fish.

But he was lonely.

Nothing in all creation seemed to be good for him. So God made one more thing.

Her name was Eve.

Do you know what was so special about these people? *They were made in the image of God.* The only thing in all creation.

Because they were made to be friends of God.

7

[fallen]

Adam and Eve lived in the Garden of Eden, a beautiful home that God gave them.

There was only one rule. One single rule. He pointed out a tree and said, "Do not eat from that tree or you will surely die."

But they did.
They disobeyed.
They weren't content.
They were greedy.

First Eve, then Adam, ate from the tree that God said "no" about, just because a snake said it was okay. The snake lied to them and they chose to believe the lie instead of God.

This was a very, very bad thing.
God was so sad. Do you know why?
Because something awful and nasty had come into His world. Something called sin.

There is a thing you should know about God: He is perfect. *That means He can't have or be in the presence of sin.*

Now both Adam and Eve, who were created to be God's friends, had sin in their lives. And God couldn't be with them anymore.

Even though God was sad, He still loved them. Oh! did He still love them!
He had a plan. And He whispered the plan into the pages of the Bible.

He told Adam and Eve that someday one of their children would fight the same snake that tricked them, and when this happened, the man would win the fight.

Adam and Eve had to leave the Garden of Eden but there was hope. Someday, somehow, God was going to fix the mess. Someday they would be free from sin.

And then, once again, they would be friends of God.

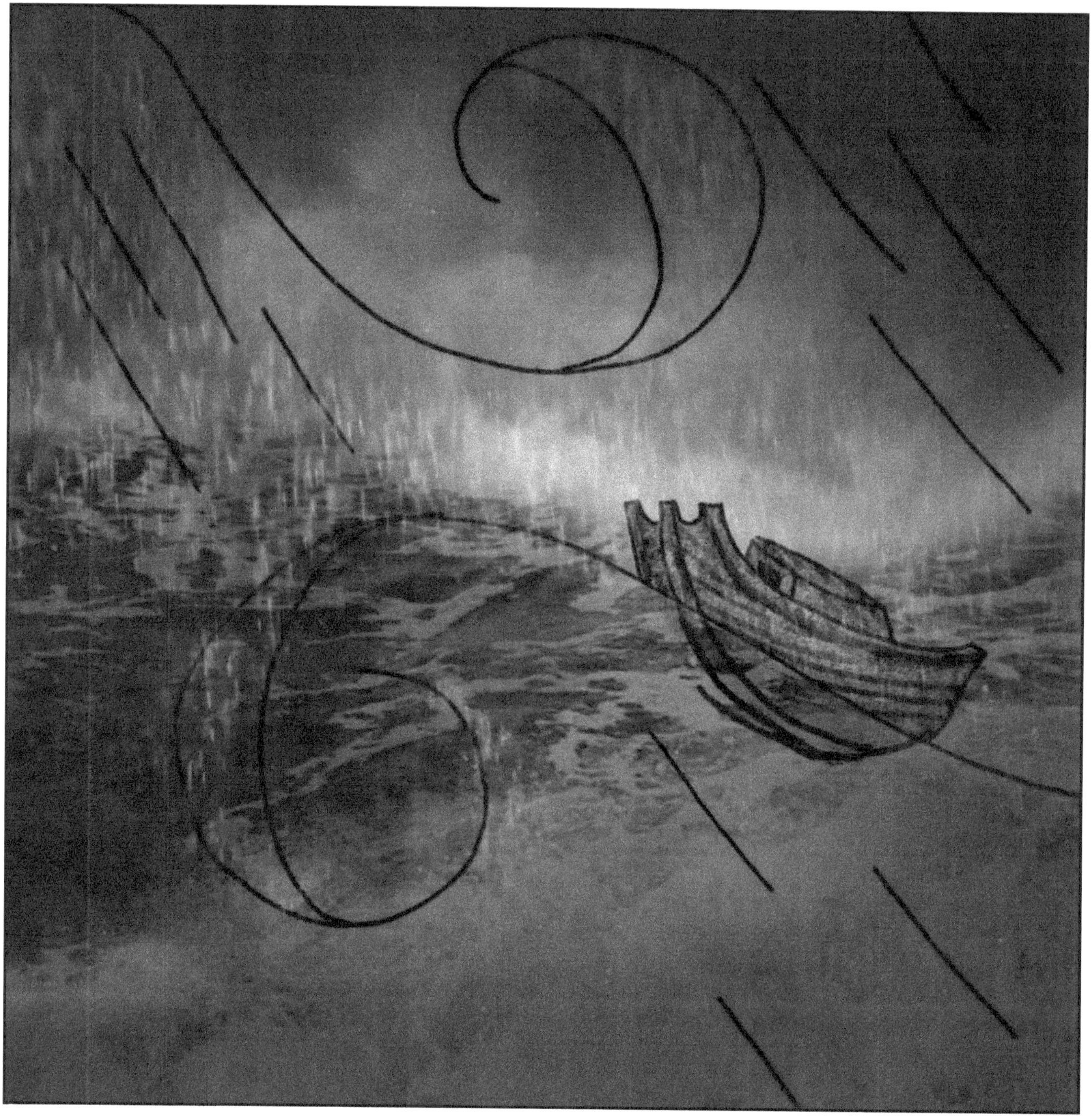

[saved]

Adam and Eve had many children. Their children had children and their children's children had children. Soon there were lots of people in the world.
But remember how Adam and Eve chose to sin instead of obeying?

Their children did too.

In fact, everyone was selfish and greedy and full of nasty sin—so much that they didn't care about God at all, even though God loved them. They made it clear that it didn't matter to them that God was making a way for them to be friends.

God was sad. Even if He could be friends with the people, they didn't want Him.

Except one man.
His name was Noah.

In all the world, he was the only man that wanted to be friends with God.

God said, "There is going to be a great flood." He told Noah to build a big boat. Then He explained that *every single person or animal in the boat* would be saved.

So Noah built. He obeyed God. Even when people laughed at him, even when people thought he was crazy.

He still obeyed.

And when the flood came, Noah and his family were the only people who went into the boat.

And they were the only ones saved.

After the flood God put a rainbow in the sky and made a promise. A very special promise. Never again would there be a great flood to cover the earth.

Noah and his family were saved by a boat, but the next time God saved all the people it would be different. The next time, they wouldn't be saved from a flood—

they would be saved from their sins.

[called]

Day Four

Sons and daughters were born to Noah's children after the flood. Soon they filled the world again. And these people, like the first people, chose to sin.

They forgot about God.
They forgot His promises.
They forgot they were made to be His friends.
Instead, they listened to the snake.

But there was one man named Abram who chose to listen to God. And God spoke!
Really great things happen when God speaks!

God told Abram to leave his country, his people and go to a new land.

And Abram listened! He didn't know where he was going or how he was going to get there. He didn't even know *why* he was going.

But he trusted God.

Abram, his wife Sarai, and all of his household went with him. They traveled for a long time. Abram sometimes did things wrong—sometimes he didn't listen to God.

Oh, but sometimes he did!

And God promised him many things. Someday, through Abram *all* the people in the *whole world* would be blessed!

God changed his name to Abraham and his wife's name to Sarah. He told Abraham to look up in the night sky. "See all those stars?" God said. "You will be the father of a people as numerous as the stars."

And one day there would be a star in the sky that would be remembered forever. A star that told the story of one of Abraham's descendants—a man God talked about way back at the beginning.

The One who would fight the snake and win. The One who would save the people from their sins. God hadn't forgotten His promise. The man was coming!

13

[offered]

Abraham and Sarah waited and waited for a child to be born like God promised.

Sometimes they were patient and sometimes they were not, *but God was faithful.* Abraham was one hundred years old and Sarah was ninety when she gave birth to their first son.

It was a miracle.

They named him Isaac and they rejoiced that God had done what He promised.
But then God did something strange. He said to Abraham, "Sacrifice your son to Me."

That didn't make sense!

Abraham could have pretended he didn't hear. Or he could have pretended to not understand. Or he could have said no. But he wanted *so desperately* to be God's friend. Even though it didn't make sense, he obeyed.

He loved God *more* than he loved his son (and that was a lot!).

Abraham took his son Isaac, the only son of the promise, and they climbed a mountain. And at the top Abraham placed Isaac on an altar. And God spoke again!

Really great things happen when God speaks!

He said, "Abraham! Now I know that you love Me because you did not withhold your only son."

Abraham looked and there was a ram caught in some thorns. Abraham and Isaac were so glad that God had provided! They sacrificed the ram instead of Isaac and they called the place, Jehovah-Jirah. (That means, *God Provides.*)

God was pleased. He said again, "Abraham, through you I will bless the whole world."
And when God did, when He blessed the whole world, we would see some of those things again:

The only son.
The sacrifice.
The thorns.

Someday, God would be Jehovah-Jirah again. He would provide a sacrifice to take our place, just like He provided the ram to take Isaac's place. *And that day, God would save the world.*

[favored]

Abraham's son Isaac grew up. He married a girl named Rebekah. Isaac and Rebekah had two sons. Jacob and Esau.

Esau was the oldest but Jacob received the birthright. (That means they treated him like he was the oldest son.) When Jacob was grown up he married two sisters. One sister, Leah, had many sons but the other sister, Rachel, didn't have any. Jacob loved Rachel the most and wanted her to have children. *Finally,* she did. A son named Joseph.

Joseph was Jacob's favorite. It's never good to have favorites and Jacob found out why!
He had eleven other sons but Jacob gave *only* Joseph a colorful coat, and this made the brothers angry. So they did something horrible. They took Joseph and sold him as a slave.

He ended up in Egypt where he had to work and work. He wasn't treated like the favorite son anymore. He wasn't even treated like a son at all. He was a slave. But something good happened!

Joseph listened to God.

He decided that he wanted to be God's friend. Once that got him thrown in jail. But Joseph still listened! And do you know what eventually happened?

He became the ruler of Egypt.

God told him some important things and used him to save the nation from starving. Joseph helped them store lots of food in the good years so there was something to eat during a famine that covered the whole country. And guess who showed up asking for food?

Joseph's brothers!

They didn't know him but Joseph knew who they were! He could have been horrible to them. But he wasn't. Instead he forgave them. He said, "You tried to do something bad, but God used it for good." His family would have starved in the famine but God used Joseph to save their lives.

Through the years in Egypt, many times things looked *really* bad. But God had a plan. *Remember?* He was making it possible for all the people in the whole world to be His friends.

[sent]

Joseph and his brothers stayed in Egypt.

Their children and grandchildren and great-great-grandchildren were called, "Israelites." Years passed and soon there were thousands of Israelites living in Egypt.

And once again, they forgot about God.

A man who didn't know Joseph became king. He was scared of the Israelites because there were so many of them. He decided to make them his slaves. It was terrible. But then something great happened.   *They remembered God!*

They prayed to Him and asked to be saved—and God heard!

God always hears when we talk to Him.

The people probably thought God was going to send someone stronger than the king to save them. But He didn't.   *He sent a baby.*

The king wanted to kill all the baby boys but God saved this baby. His mother put him in a basket and hid him in the grass in the river. Guess who found him? *A princess!* She named him Moses. He was adopted and became a prince! It sure seemed like God would use Moses to save the people then, but He didn't. First, Moses did something terrible. He tried to save the Israelites all by himself and instead, *he killed a man and ran away.* It was very, very bad. *But God still loved Moses* and the people still needed someone to save them.

Moses became a shepherd, out in the wilderness. He thought he was hiding. But God knew where Moses was. And God spoke.

Really great things happen when God speaks.

Moses saw something crazy weird. A bush was on fire *but it didn't burn up!* It was God! He said, "Moses! My people are crying for help. Go now because I am setting them free."

Moses was scared. He had tried to help the Israelites before and that had turned out badly. But this time God was the one doing the work. Moses didn't want to go *but he did.* He went because God said so. Because God was working. Because God had a plan, *just like He said,* from the very beginning.

[covered]

Moses went back to Egypt and his brother Aaron went with him. They went to the King and said, "God says to let the Israelite people go."

Do you know what the King said?

He said, "No!"

The people were his slaves and he didn't want to let them leave. No matter what Moses and Aaron said, the King wouldn't listen.

The King thought that he was more powerful than God.

So God did some pretty crazy things. They were called "plagues." He did them to remind the King that *no one* is more powerful than God.

Each time Moses went before the King and asked for the Israelites to be set free, the King would say, "No", and another plague would come.

God made water turn into blood. Frogs came from the river. Gnats flew everywhere. Flies swarmed. Animals died. People had sores. Hail came. Locusts flew in. And it got very, very dark.

And still, after each plague, the King said, *"No!"*

So finally, the very worst thing happened. God said, "Every family that doesn't have blood from a perfect lamb on the top and sides of their doorpost will lose their oldest son."

This was something sad and hard. God gave them *so* many chances to listen.

But they didn't.

The only way to be saved was with blood in the shape of a cross, and the King did not use it.

The King was so, so sad when his son died. He told the Israelites, "Go!"
So the people left. They followed Moses out of Egypt.

For the first time, people were saved by blood and a cross.
But it wouldn't be the last.

[guided]

Moses led the Israelites out of Egypt. They came to a big lake called *The Red Sea.*
They looked back and saw the Egyptian King was coming after them with a huge army! The people were so scared. *They forgot about how God had just saved them.* They turned to Moses and said, "We're going to die!" But Moses didn't forget. He talked to God.

Remember, God always hears when we talk to Him.

And then it happened. God spoke.

Really great things happen when God speaks.

He said, "Moses, hold up your staff."

Moses listened and the water in the Red Sea started moving! A wind blew and a path opened, *right through the middle of the water!* The people walked across on dry ground but when the Egyptians tried to come after them, the water crashed down.

God had saved His people *again.*

Over and over, God saved them.

Even when they didn't listen to Him.
Even when they turned away from Him.
Even when they forgot Him.
Because God is faithful.

They traveled into the desert. It was hot, and dry. They were thirsty, and they were so very hungry. Do you know what happened? *The people forgot how God took care of them.*

They cried to Moses saying, "Did you bring us here to starve in the desert?" So Moses talked to God and in the morning, when the people walked outside their tents, they found something on the ground. It was white and small and tasted like honey. They called it *manna.*

Every morning they went out and gathered enough manna to feed them for the day. It only lasted one day, but it was there every morning. *A miracle.* Every day another miracle.

They were made to be God's friends, and God was teaching them how to trust Him, so that when the sin was taken care of, those who knew God could walk with Him again.

23

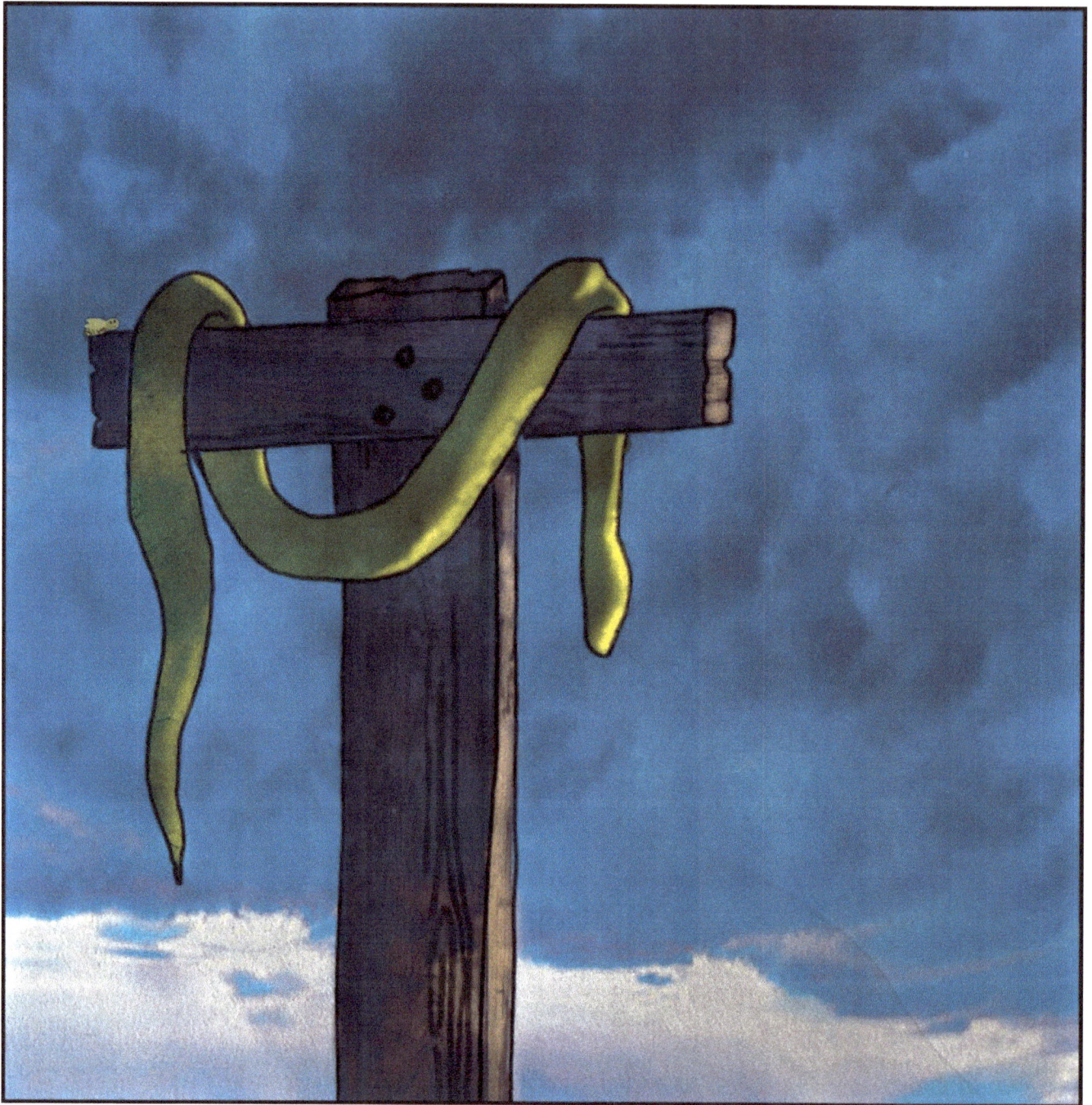

[reminded]

The Israelites were living in the desert. God provided food and water. He gave them a cloud to lead them during the day and a pillar of fire to guide them at night.

He took care of them.

But the people were not thankful.
They grumbled. They complained. They moaned.
"We don't like the desert. We don't like this manna. We want to go back to Egypt!"

It is a very bad thing to not be thankful. God was working to make a way for them to be friends and they didn't care. They wanted more than what God had given them. *Just like Adam and Eve in the garden.* The people couldn't see him but the snake was back. He was whispering, *"God isn't really good. He's not really taking care of you. He's not giving you what you need."*

If they would have looked around they could have seen that God was taking care of them. It was obvious that He was good. *But they didn't look.*

Instead, they listened to the snake.

So God sent live slithering snakes among them. They were poisonous. They bit the people and many became sick and died. It was so sad. But something good happened! The people remembered how God had saved them before. They asked Moses to pray, to talk to God and see if He would save them again.

Remember, God always hears when we talk to Him!

God told Moses to make a bronze snake and put it up on a pole. When the people got bit by a snake, *they just had to look up.* Nothing more. Just look at the snake on the pole. And if they did, they were healed.

A miracle.

It was a reminder of the promise, the one from the very beginning. *Someone was coming.* Someone who would fight the snake *and win.* This man would be lifted up, just like the snake on the pole was lifted, and all people would need to do is look to Him and *they would be healed.* Sins forgiven. Friendship with God possible.

A miracle.

[commanded]

Even after the miracle of food and water and protection. Even after the snakes. Even after all the promises. The people forgot. *They just kept forgetting about God.* God wanted to meet with them. To talk to them. To walk with them. He loved them.

But the people didn't love Him back.

One day, God invited everyone to talk to Him. All the people. But they were afraid of meeting with God, so only Moses went. God sent a message back to the Israelites. He wrote it on two stone tablets. The very first thing He said was, "I am your God…" Then He gave them a list. Ten simple things to do or not to do.

No other gods.	No murdering.
No idols.	No adultery.
No swearing.	No stealing.
Keep the Sabbath.	No lying.
Honor your parents.	No coveting.

But remember when God gave Adam and Eve one simple rule?   *They disobeyed.*

Well, the Israelites did too. All those good rules to keep them safe and take care of them, they broke. God knew they would. But God made the rules anyway. He gave them as a reminder that *the people were sinners*. They had to remember that. Because if they forgot, if they just kept doing wrong things and forgot about God, if they thought they were "good enough" to be saved when they still had all that sin inside–*then they wouldn't look.*

When the man came to fight the snake and save them from sin, they wouldn't look, and they wouldn't be healed. There wouldn't be a miracle, and they would never be God's friends.

And that would break God's heart.

So He made laws. Laws so they could see when they sinned. Laws so they would know they needed help. Laws so when the time came they would *look* because they knew how desperately they needed a Savior.

[accepted]

The Israelites wandered in the desert for forty years. God tried to give them a home—but they were too scared.

They forgot how great God was.
So they stayed in the desert.

After Moses died, a man named Joshua became the leader. Joshua didn't forget. He knew God was strong enough to do anything He said. Joshua sent spies into the land God said would be their home. A land called *Canaan.*

The spies went into a great city called Jericho. It had a big wall all around it. While they were in the city they went to a woman's house. Her name was Rahab.

The King of Jericho sent her a message. It said, "Bring me the men who came to you, they are spies!"

But Rahab hid the men instead.

She told them, "I know your God has given you this land. I've heard all about the miracles. About the Red Sea. About how He's saved you over and over. I believe He is the true God. Please save me and my family." She didn't doubt God's power. She knew how strong He was.

The men agreed. They said, "You must put this scarlet cord in your window and all your family must stay in your house with you." Rahab listened. She tied the scarlet cord in her window.

When the Israelite people fought against Jericho, they won—just like God promised. He used a miracle to make the big wall fall down and all the people in the city died. The spies went looking and found Rahab and her family alive and safe inside the house with the scarlet cord.

Just like the cross of blood on the doors in Egypt, the red cord marked Rahab as one who believed. She believed in God's power. She heard the stories of His miracles and believed that He was *strong enough* and *good enough* to save her. She wanted to be God's friend. And He accepted her.

God did for Rahab what He wants to do for the whole world, He saved her.

[redeemed]

Day Thirteen

Rahab had a son named Boaz. He was a good man who wanted to follow God.
He lived in a town called Bethlehem.

One day he was out in his fields and he saw a young woman gleaning grain. He asked about her and his servant said, "She is Naomi's daughter-in-law, Ruth." Boaz knew about Naomi. She and her husband had left Bethlehem years before with their two sons. They went to Moab.

Moab was not a good place.
The people there did not follow God.

Naomi's husband and sons all died there. When Naomi came back to Bethlehem, she was a widow. Her son Mahlon had married a girl named Ruth, and even though he had died too, Ruth stayed with Naomi. She told her mother-in-law, *"I believe in your God."* She left her country, her family, her friends—

just so she could know God.

But Ruth and Naomi needed someone to help them. They were very poor. Some of the Israelites didn't like people from other places like Moab, *but not Boaz*. Remember, his mom was from Jericho!

Boaz gave Ruth and Naomi food and tried to help them as much as he could, but he wanted to do more. Then Ruth came to Boaz. "Will you take care of me?" she asked. Boaz was so glad!

He married her, gave her his name, bought back her land.
He gave her a safe place to live, loved her, redeemed her.

After they were married Ruth had a son named Obed. Now Naomi and Ruth had family.
Boaz did for Ruth the same thing that God wants to do for His people.

Save them, give them His name, give them a safe home.
Make them family, love them, redeem them.
And all they have to do is ask.

31

[anointed]

Ruth and Boaz had a grandson named Jesse.

Jesse had eight sons. The youngest was named David. He was a shepherd who took care of sheep. One day he was called in from the fields to meet a man named Samuel, who told him to kneel down. *Samuel anointed him as the next King of Israel.*

Everyone wondered, "Why him?" David wasn't the tallest or strongest or best looking. He wasn't the smartest or quickest. He was just a kid! And God spoke.
Really great things happen when God speaks.

God said, "I don't see the same way people see. People look at the outside of a person, but I look at the heart." *In his heart, David wanted to be friends with God.*

He didn't become king right away. He went back to his fields and his sheep. While he was still young, an army came against Israel. There was a huge giant who would laugh at the soldiers. "Choose someone to fight me!" He would say.

The soldiers were scared. They looked at the enormous giant-man and forgot about God's power. But David didn't. He visited the battlefield and heard the giant, Goliath, laughing.

He looked at Goliath and said, "How can this man defy the army of the living God?" He knew it wasn't just the people Goliath was laughing at. The giant was laughing at God Himself. David believed that God was the strongest of all. He went and got five smooth stones for his sling-shot.

The big giant got angry. "You sent a boy to fight me?" He hollered. But David looked right at him. "You will lose," he said, "because I fight *for God*, by *God's power*." He took five stones—
but he only used one.

David won the battle. Not because he was the biggest or strongest or smartest. He won because he fought on God's side and God always wins.

And someday, *someday*, a man would come fight the biggest, scariest giant of all—that terrible liar of a snake—and just like God promised, He would win.

[obedient]

Many years passed in Israel and many people chose to not remember God.
But there were some people who *did* remember Him! And God noticed.

There was a man who followed God who died and left behind a widow and two sons. The widow was so poor that she couldn't pay her bills. Some of the people she owed money to were demanding she pay. The widow did the only thing she knew to do. She went to a man named Elisha to ask for help.

Elisha was a prophet. A prophet was someone who listened to God and told the people what God said. When the widow asked for help, Elisha listened and God spoke.
Really great things happen when God speaks.

Elisha told the woman, "Go; get all the containers you can find."
The woman and her sons did what the prophet said. They believed God would help them. When they had gathered all the containers Elisha said, "Go inside your house, take your jar of oil and start filling the containers."

That sounded pretty crazy! They only had *one* jar of oil and there were *a lot* of containers!

But they listened to God.

They picked up that one little container and started pouring the oil into the new containers. Oil kept coming and coming and coming, until *every* jar was full!
It was a miracle!

Because when God wants something to multiply—nothing can stop it. And when God speaks—miracles happen. And what He says *is* even if it wasn't. And even though it looked like God had forgotten His promise to send someone to fight the snake and save the people—*He hadn't.*

Even when the people couldn't see it, God was working to make it possible for every person to be His friend again.

35

[written]

There was a man named Isaiah. He wanted to be God's friend and he wanted to help others be friends of God too.

But most of the people didn't care about God. They didn't want to listen to Him. Instead, they wanted to live however they pleased, without following any rules or being friends with God.

But God still loved them.
He wanted to talk to them, so one day God asked, "Who should I send? Who will tell the people what I say?"

Isaiah said, "Me! I will go!"

So God told him, "Tell the people they have sinned. They do so many wrong things. They need to be healed, and I want to heal them! But they don't want to be healed."

Isaiah felt sad. Why didn't the people want to be healed of their sin? He asked God, "How long will it be like this?" And God spoke.
Really great things happen when God speaks!

"It will be a long time. But when it seems like all hope is gone, *my promise will still be there.*"
And then God told the secret again. He said, "People who are lost in sinful darkness—*will see a great light!* Those who are living in the shadow of death (the shadow caused by sin)—*will have light dawn in their lives!*"

Isaiah got so excited! He wrote down what God said so *everyone, everywhere* could know!
He wrote, "A child will be born! A son! And he will be called:
Wonderful Counselor, Mighty God,
Everlasting Father, Prince of Peace."

This wasn't just any child—*God was talking about the promise!* The one from the beginning. God didn't forget, even though the people forgot Him.
The man was coming to fight the snake!

[forgiven]

Even after all the promises, even after all the times that God spoke, and all the really great things that happened, the people still refused to listen to God.

But there was a man named Hosea who did listen to God. He was a prophet.

One day, God told Hosea to marry a woman named Gomer. Hosea obeyed. He married her and loved her. *But she ran away.*

She did! It was so sad. And God told Hosea, "This is the same thing that the people have done to Me. I've loved them, and they've run away from Me." Then God told Hosea, "Go, find your wife and bring her home."

So Hosea went and found his wife. He brought her home and loved her, even though she had hurt him so badly. And then, she ran away again. *It was so, so sad.* Hosea was devastated. He was hurt.

It was the same thing the people did to God. God loved them and they ran away. God brought them back and loved them—and they ran away again. They just kept forgetting God. It made God *so* sad. But what would happen now? Hosea had loved his wife and brought her home, and she had run away a second time! Would Hosea *and God* just find someone else to love? I bet Hosea wanted to, but God spoke.

Really great things happen when God speaks!

God said, "Go save your wife."

This time Gomer had gotten in so much trouble, she was a slave! And Hosea went and paid to set her free. He paid the price so that she didn't have to be a slave anymore. And he loved her still.

God reminded everyone of the promise, *again.* The people were in so much trouble! They were slaves to sin. And God promised, *I'm going to pay the price to set you free.* Because even though the people had hurt God—God loved them still.

He wanted them to be His friends.

[concerned]

Nineveh was a city filled with people who did not love or serve God.

But God loved them.

God told one of His prophets, a man named Jonah, to go and warn the people that their city was going to be destroyed. Do you know what Jonah did? He tried to run away.

Of course, it didn't work.

Jonah found out that no one can hide from God. He was on a ship when a terrible storm came. Jonah told the sailors to throw him into the sea so they could be saved. When they did, the storm stopped and God sent a big fish to swallow Jonah.

But Jonah didn't die.

He lived inside that smelly, yucky fish for three days and three nights. While he was inside the fish, Jonah repented for trying to disobey God. The fish vomited Jonah onto the shore and Jonah went to Nineveh like God said. He told all those bad people that God was not happy.

Do you know what the people did? They believed God. They said they were sorry. They changed what they were doing. They listened to Him.

And God forgave them!

You would think Jonah would have been super happy!

But he wasn't.
He was mad.

He didn't want the people in Nineveh to be forgiven. He thought they deserved to die.

One day God made a vine grow. It gave Jonah shade from the hot sun. Then, in one day, the vine died. Jonah was so mad! He liked that vine, and now it was gone!

God said, "Jonah! You're upset about a vine, which you didn't create or work for, and you wonder why I am concerned about all the many people in Nineveh?"

It was the very deepest truth: God is concerned about His people. And one day a man would come and he would face death for three days and three nights, like Jonah did in the belly of the fish. And like Jonah, this man would come out! And everyone, the people in Nineveh, and even you and me, would get a chance to be friends with God.

[protected]

The Israelite people kept forgetting to listen to God, so a big army came against them.

The people were captured and taken to a city called *Babylon.* One of them was a man named Daniel who worked hard to not forget God again. Every day, three times a day, he opened his window and knelt down and prayed.
Remember, God always hears when we talk to Him.

Daniel wanted to be friends with God. He trusted that God loved him and would take care of him.
And God did!

Daniel was honored in Babylon. He was even friends with the King! But there were some very bad men who didn't like Daniel. They made a plan to get rid of him. They went to the King and said, "Oh, King, you are so powerful and so great. Make a law that for thirty days the people must worship and pray only to you—or they will be thrown in the lion's den."

This was very bad. What was Daniel going to do? If he opened his window and prayed to God then he would be fed to hungry lions.
But Daniel had courage.

Do you know what he did? He opened his window and prayed. He knew God was the most powerful, the greatest, and the most wonderful in the entire world. God was God. The King was not God.
And only God should be worshiped.

Those bad men were watching. They took Daniel to the King. The King was so sad! He did not think before he made the law. Now Daniel had to be fed to the lions.

Daniel was taken and lowered down into the den of hungry beasts. But do you want to know a secret?
Nothing, in all the world, is as strong as God.
Not even hungry lions.

The next morning the King said, "Daniel! Has your God protected you?" And Daniel answered, "Yes!" There is only one God. Just one. *And He is the greatest and strongest of all.* Nothing, not one single thing, can beat God. Not kings. Not bad men. Not lions. Not snakes. *Nothing.*

[surprised]

Years and years passed. Eventually a man named Zechariah lived in Jerusalem. He had a wife named Elizabeth but no children.

This made them very sad.

They were married for many years and it looked like they would never be parents.
Then one day, while Zechariah was in the temple, God spoke.

Really great things happen when God speaks.

God said through an angel named Gabriel, "Your wife Elizabeth will bear a son and you will name him John."

But Zechariah had forgotten, just like the Israelite people kept forgetting. He forgot how BIG God was. He forgot that nothing is stronger than God. So he didn't believe. He said, "How can I be sure of this? I'm old and my wife is old."

He forgot that age doesn't matter to God.
He forgot that God can do anything.
He forgot how good and loving God is.

So Gabriel said to him, "I came here right from God, to tell you the good things God says. Now, you won't be able to speak until this thing happens because you did not believe me."

And he couldn't.
Zechariah couldn't talk at all.

But guess what? It happened. Elizabeth became pregnant! She had a little boy and when Zechariah named the baby John, he could finally speak again.

It was such a surprise!
But it should not have been.
God made a promise to Eve, at the very beginning of time, and God always keeps his promises. He always does what He says He will do. *Something wonderful was going to happen.*

God's promise was coming.

[chosen]

Elizabeth had a relative named Mary.
She lived in a town called Nazareth and was engaged to marry a man named Joseph.

One day, before the two were married, an angel appeared to her.

She was pretty scared!

But the angel said, "Mary, don't be afraid!" The angel told her something glorious. It was a message from God. The angel said to her, "You will have a son and you will name Him Jesus. He will be great and will be called the Son of God."

Mary didn't know what to think! She wasn't even married, *how could she have a baby?* So she asked the angel and he said, "The Holy Spirit will come upon you."

This wasn't just an ordinary baby. *This was the promise!*
Mary told the angel, "May it be as you have said."

And God was pleased.

But her fiancé, Joseph, was sad. He thought Mary had not been faithful to him. He was a good man, so he planned to break their engagement quietly. But the angel showed up again. And God spoke.

Really great things happen when God speaks.

The angel told him, "Joseph, don't be afraid to take Mary home as your wife." The angel explained who the baby was, that His name would be Jesus, and they would call Him, *Emmanuel.*
(Emmanuel means, *God with us.*)

Oh, oh! It wasn't just any man who was coming—it was God, Himself!

He was coming because He loved.
He wanted the people to be His friends.

Just like He promised, from the very beginning, someone would fight the snake. All those years the people wondered and waited, looking for the man who would save them all.

They had no idea that it would be God, Himself.

[born]

There was a man named Augustus, who was Caesar (that's like a king).

Augustus wanted to know how many people lived in his country. He made a rule that everyone had to return to their hometown and register.

This was called a census.

Mary and Joseph had to travel to a town called Bethlehem. By the time they got there, Mary was ready to have her baby.

When they arrived, all the inns were full right up! Place after place turned them away.

Poor Mary.

Finally, they found a stable where they could stay. A stable is where animals are kept, and that's where Mary had her baby. She wrapped Him up in strips of cloth and laid Him in a manger.

Her baby was God, Himself.

God could have been born anywhere.
A palace. A warm house. A clean bed.
But He chose a stable.

He didn't come to make Himself great.

He came to fight the snake. *To show His love.* To make it possible for us to be His friends.

Just like the angel said, Jesus came to be Emmanuel.
God, right here, *with us.*

Most of the people didn't know He was there. They had no idea God had come to earth as a baby. They were still busy forgetting about Him.

But God came anyway.

He gave up all the wonderful things in the heavens to come right down to earth. He came to fight for the friendship of all people.

He came because He loved.

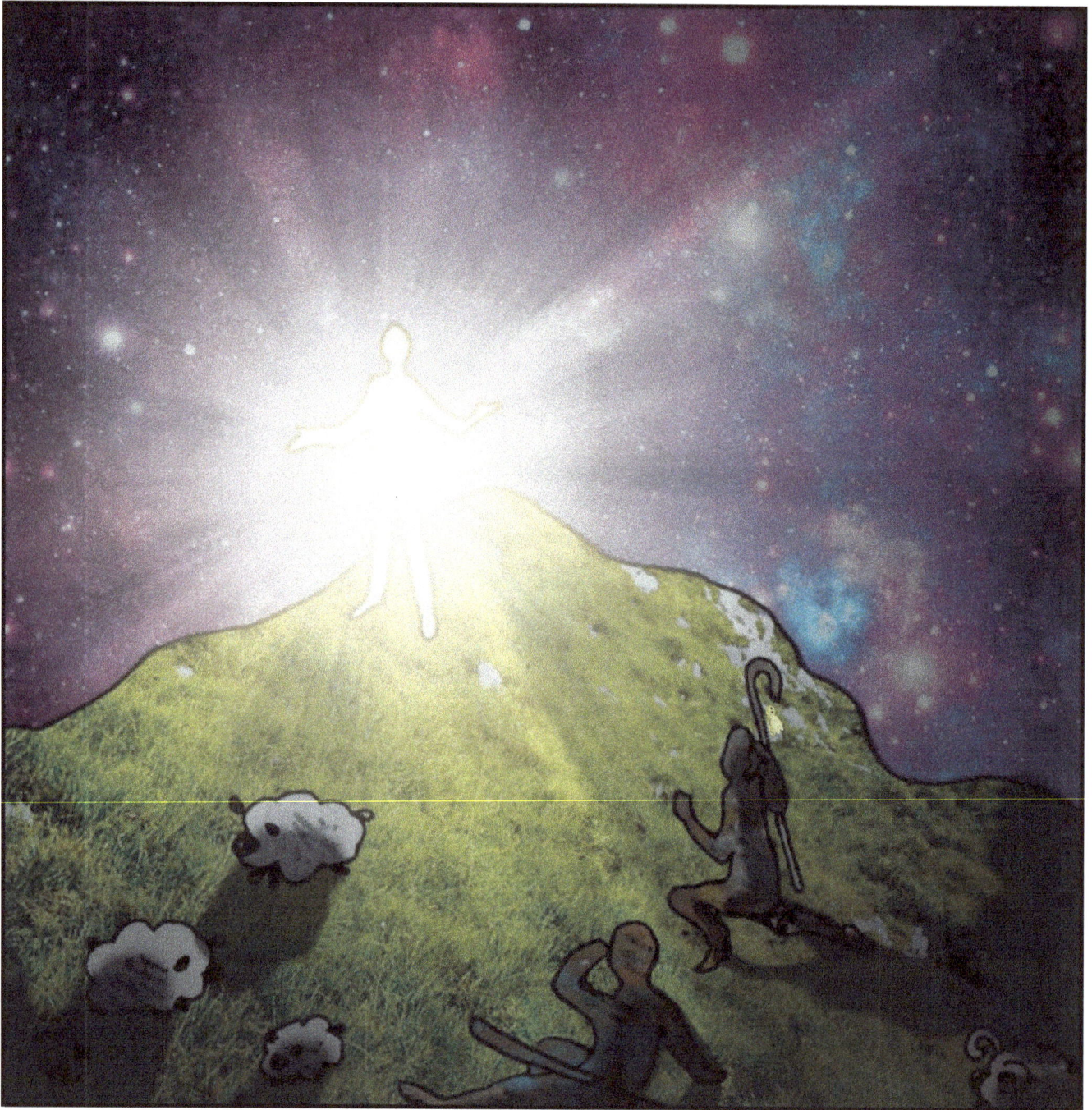

[announced]

On the hills outside Bethlehem there were shepherds.
(Shepherds were people who watched over sheep.) They spent a lot of quiet nights in the hills.

The shepherds didn't know it at first, but this wasn't just any night.
This was a special night.

> *It was the night Jesus was born.*
> *It was the night God came to be with us.*

While the shepherds were there in the hills with their sheep, an angel appeared! It must have scared them a lot!

The angel said, "Don't be afraid! I bring you wonderful news! Joyful news! Today in Bethlehem a Savior has been born to you. He is Christ the Lord."

The shepherds were trying to decide what to do about this when suddenly! There were many, many angels there! They were all praising God saying,

> *Glory to God in the highest*
> *And on earth peace to men on whom His favor rests!*

They were giving glory to God for this wonderful gift. This promise come true.

> *This baby who had come to fight the snake.*

The shepherds were excited! After all those years. After all the good days and bad days. After all the prophets and preachers. After all the kings who loved God and the kings who didn't. The Savior was finally here!

They decided to go find Jesus. They went to Bethlehem and found Mary and Joseph and the baby. *It was just like the angel said.* They were in a stable, with the baby wrapped in cloth and lying in a manger. They were so excited they told everyone they met about Jesus. About the Savior. About Emmanuel, *God with us.*

The One who had come to make it possible for us to be friends of God.

[given]

There were some Wise Men who lived in the East. They knew how to read the stars.
Crazy, I know!

When Jesus was born, God sent a special sign, *a new star*. It was like a note in the sky that said,
"Hey, I'm here! It's Me, the King of kings."

And the Wise Men could read it! It was like God speaking right to them. And we know—
Really great things happen when God speaks.

The men traveled a long time over a great distance. Eventually they ended up in Bethlehem. When they got there they didn't know where the house was that Jesus lived. So they went to a man named Herod, the ruler of the Jewish people, and asked him.

Herod was *so* upset. He was the king but these men said a new king had been born! He pretended to be nice to the Wise Men, hoping to eventually find out where Jesus was so he could kill Him. "When you find the boy, come tell me where He is…" Herod said.

It was like the snake knew his time was almost up.
He wanted so desperately to get rid of Jesus.

When the Wise Men found Jesus, they knelt down and worshiped him. They knew exactly who He was. Emmanuel, God with us. The promise, come to life. The One who would make it possible for us to be friends with God.

The Wise Men brought Him gifts. They brought Him: gold, frankincense, and myrrh.
These were expensive, special gifts. And Jesus was worthy of them.
And it's just the same today. He is worthy of everything we have. Everything we are.

When the Wise Men went to leave, an angel appeared to them in a dream and told them not to go back to Herod. They obeyed and went home a different way. This made Herod angry, but even though he tried to find and kill Jesus, he couldn't. The day was coming when Jesus would fight the battle with the snake. *But not yet.*

[loved]

Day Twenty-Five

At Christmas we celebrate the birth of Jesus—but the reason we celebrate isn't just that He was born.

It's also that He died.

Remember that snake?
Remember the promise?
Jesus was the man that God promised. The One who would fight the snake and win.

First He grew and grew. He went from being a baby to being an adult. And in all that time He never sinned.

Not once.

He was perfect and lived like Adam and Eve should have all those years ago.
But the people didn't realize it was God. They forgot about the promises and they didn't believe what the angels and miracles said: that this was Emmanuel.

So they nailed Him to a cross. They killed Jesus.

And the snake thought he had won.
He thought that God was dead.

But God wasn't dead.
Not even a little.

It was all part of the promise. It was all part of the plan God had written down in the pages of the Bible. It was God working to make it possible for us to be His friends.

Remember the sheep that took Isaac's place? *It died for him.*
The blood on the doors in Egypt? *It dripped in the shape of a cross.*
The red cord on Rahab's window? *The color of blood.*
The snake on a pole in the desert? *Looking up saved the people.*
The promise of being redeemed like Ruth, and the promise of light from Isaiah.

It was all part of the plan from the very beginning.

You see, there was something the snake didn't know:

will comfort them,
make them rejoice
rather than sorrow.
satiate the soul of the
with abundance,
people shall be
Prosperity of Judah
says the LORD of hosts,
of Israel: "They shall again
speech in the land of Judah
its cities, when I bring back
captivity: "The LORD bless

Death came from sin,
and a sinless man cannot die.

So do you know what happened? After the people killed Jesus, His Spirit went right down into hell, fought the snake *and won.*

We know because three days later, He rose up from the dead.

Death has no power over the sinless.

So what about us?
What about all the people in the whole world that God created to be His friends?

We can be.
Just like God promised.

Remember?

There is blood. *Blood pays the debt of sin.*
There is a cross. *Jesus died on the cross, not because of His sin but because of yours.*
There is love. *He loves you and longs to be your friend.*
There is redemption. *He wants to set you free from death.*

In fact, God spoke to us through the Bible and tells us what to do.

And we know that really great things happen when God speaks.

He said, "If you confess with your mouth that Jesus is Lord,
And believe in your heart that God raised him from the dead;

YOU WILL BE SAVED."

That's all we have to do and just like He promised, *we'll become friends of God.*

Learn More!

Day 1: Genesis 1

Day 2: Genesis 3

Day 3: Genesis 6

Day 4: Genesis 12:1-9, Genesis 15:5

Day 5: Genesis 22:1-19

Day 6: Genesis 37, Genesis 44-45

Day 7: Exodus 3

Day 8: Exodus 7:14-11:10

Day 9: Exodus 14, Exodus 15-16

Day 10: Numbers 21:4-9

Day 11: Deuteronomy 5

Day 12: Joshua 2, Joshua 6:22-23

Day 13: Ruth 1-4

Day 14: I Samuel 17

Day 15: 2 Kings 4:1-7

Day 16: Isaiah 6:8, Isaiah 9:2-7

Day 17: Hosea 1, Hosea 3

Day 18: Jonah 1, Jonah 3

Day 19: Daniel 6

Day 20: Luke 1:5-25, 57-66

Day 21: Luke 1:26-38,
         Matthew 1:18-24

Day 22: Luke 2:1-7

Day 23: Luke 2:8-20

Day 24: Matthew 2:1-12

Day 25: Luke 23:26-49,
         Luke 24:1-12
         2 Corinthians 5:21

Author

Natasha Metzler lives on a farm in Northern New York with her husband, two children, and whatever animals her daughter talks them into adopting.

Her heart's desire is to share the love of Jesus with as many people as she can.

She is the author of several books, including *Pain Redeemed*, and can be found online at natashametzler.com

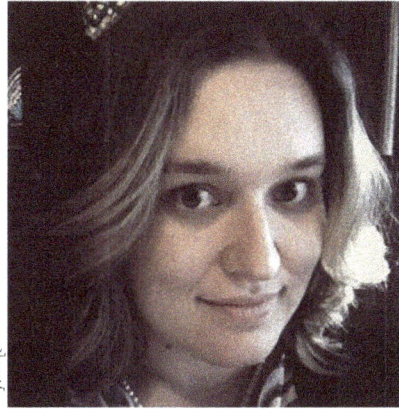

Illustrator

Brianna Siegrist is a writer, artist, mother, and wife. She spends her days homesteading with her husband and three children and is learning to wrangle Red Angus cattle, though she'd rather paint them.

Using her gifts to teach children about the love of God is a major part of her life's calling.

She is the author of *The Next Chef*, and can be found online at briannasiegrist.wordpress.com

www.ingramcontent.com/pod-product-compliance
Lightning Source LLC
Chambersburg PA
CBHW060802150426
42813CB00059B/2846